Hello Survivor!

by

Sheri D. Smith

Unless otherwise indicated,
Scripture quotations are from the King James Version
of the Bible.

HELLO SURVIVOR

Copyright © 2020 by Sheri D. Smith

ISBN: 978-0-9787118-1-8

For information contact:

Sheri D. Smith

sheridsmith@hotmail.com

TABLE OF CONTENTS

DEDICATION

I dedicate this book to my Lord and Savior Jesus

Christ. To God be the Glory. I thank Him for His

Divine purpose in making me who I am today.

God has delivered unto me a message for Survivors

In this season. Thank you JESUS!

ACKNOWLEDGEMENTS

To my loving children who are my hearts. Shaquita and Deonte I love you with all my heart. Thank you for being supportive of me. Also, in loving memory of my dear love Chantez (Son), who I know would be smiling about the completion of this book. I Love you and miss you!

Mother, my Queen thank you for giving me life. I Honor you and love you very much. Because of You mother, I am a fighter. God bless you Queen!

To my siblings, Carolyn, Keith and Princess. Thank You for your support. Thank you for being there when I needed you the most. All of you ROCK! I love you dearly!

INTRODUCTION

As you read this book, you will realize that it is not over until God say it is over. All the haters in the world cannot stop Gods plans for your life. God's word says in the book of Jeremiah 29:11, "I know the plans I have for you." "Plans to prosper you and not to harm you." "Plans to give you hope and a future." This lets me know that God can shower us with success and blessings in life.

It also lets me know that God has a purpose for suffering. Now you could not have told me this years ago, but today is a new day. Apply your own personal experiences as you read the message. Take hold of it, struggle with it, apply it to your own life, test it, challenge it or discuss it. Go ahead and involve yourself in this book.

Let me tell you something. God is a just God. And no matter how bad the situation looks, you can always come out on top with God on your side. Listen, God wants you to survive this season. I have been taught the importance of survival. Instead of complaining about struggles, I use them to fuel my success. Anything in your life that was created to take you down or keep you down is going to be a steppingstone to take you higher.

If you want an uncommon move of God, you must do something uncommon. You must do something new. God is doing a new thing this season. Come on now. God is doing something brand new through you. Something that has not been seen or done yet. You may have tried to work your own plans. So, if your plans don't workout, don't worry God has better ones. You can depend on God. Don't spend another sleepless night worrying because God is working it out. Let's pray for each other and watch God change things.

Nobody or nothing can stop God. No sickness, no addiction, no bad break because God has the final say. This is a new season. God is about to do a new thing. Sometimes we hurt ourselves by picking up things God told us to put down. Note to self in this season, don't pick up what God told you to put down.

What am I talking about? I'm glad you asked that question. Don't pick up weights, distractions or hindrances to name a few. Be careful not to allow your heart to get in the way of these things.

You got this! John 1:46 says, "Nazareth! Can anything good come from there?" Nathaniel asked. "Come and see," said Philip. Let people come and see that you did not give up or throw in the towel. Let them come and see that you are still here despite your storms or circumstances.

Come on and show me what you're working with. I don't know about you but where I am from, I decree and declare that something good comes from here.

I decree and declare that I am that good thing. We can't go wrong with God on our side. Scripture also says, "Thou shalt also decree a thing, and it shall be established unto thee." Job 22:28.

In other words, **"SAY SOMETHING!"** Speak over yourself! I'm about to speak some good stuff over my life. I mean positive things and not negative. I'm talking about speaking life and not death over myself. I suggest you do the same thing. I say that because words have power.

Isaiah 43:19 says, "Behold, I will do a new thing; now it shall spring forth; shall you not know it? I will even make a way in the wilderness, and rivers in the desert."

Get ready for God to show up and show out! God is calling you, equipping you and preparing you according to His purpose. I can't wait for your new thing to spring forth.

- THAT GIRL -

To the girl that survived a terminal illness.

To the girl that lost a child.

To the girl that was in an unhealthy relationship.

To the girl that slept on her apartment floor because she couldn't afford furniture.

To the girl that lived paycheck to paycheck.

To the girl that was talked about because of her employment.

To the girl that foreclosed on her home.

To the girl that got her lights cut off.

To the girl that had to use the food pantry from time to time

To the girl that did caretaking for family members.

To the girl who was rejected many times because she just didn't fit in.

To the girl that cried and prayed many times expecting a miracle to happen.

I SEE YOU! I FEEL YOU!

I am that girl. I am here to let you know that you deserve joy and happiness. Don't quit! Don't give up! Don't you dare worry about anybody that has a problem with where you work when they are not paying your rent, mortgage or bills point blank and let me add the period. There are a lot of people that voice their opinions but not willing to help you. Trust me when I say that God is big and bad enough to remove that job when or if He is ready for you to leave it. Hello somebody! I am a witness to that. I am sick and tired of being sick and tired! Please, please keep it moving. We're depending on you not only to Survive but Thrive! Girl, some don't understand until they have walked in your shoes. Keep marching on Girl! You got this!

- THAT GIRL -

CHAPTER 1

Hello Survivor!

Most people think of Breast Cancer or some other form of cancer when you say the word Survivor. Yes, I am a Breast Cancer Survivor since my diagnosis of 2010. I was devastated by the diagnosis. The chemo and radiation were no fun at all. I was so weak in my body. I would collapse at times. I didn't want to eat, and I lost all my beautiful long hair. Even though the Doctor told me that I would lose my hair, I told the Doctor that I will not lose my hair, but I did anyway.

Each day my hair was falling out until I was completely bald. That devastated me! But God! The diagnosis from the Doctor is never final! Why?

Because we serve a powerful God that miraculously heals! I certainly thank my God for me being cancer free. It was a process, but God did it! And He is still working on me today in other areas of my life!

The day I received the news of my diagnosis, was the day that my whole life changed. I remember sitting in the office with my mother and sister when the Doctor gave me the news.

When he said you have Breast Cancer, I just looked at him in silence. I couldn't say anything at the time. I was shocked! I sat there and watched him as he continued to tell me what was next. Tears were in his eyes.

I turned and I looked at my mother and sister and tears were in their eyes. I was feeling like, "No this doesn't mean it's over!" "Everything will be okay!" Let this journey begin. "I don't know why I am here in this place or situation but let's deal with it."

Let's move forward with an attitude that I will be okay. After looking at all the expressions on each of their faces, then the Doctor says to me, "You are strong." "You will be okay." He then smiled. I found out later that his wife was dealing with Breast Cancer at the same time I received my diagnosis. Wow! No wonder he had tears in his eyes when giving me my diagnosis, I thought.

The day of my surgery, I went to the hospital with a good attitude and was even joking around with my family and the Doctor. I chose the Lumpectomy surgery. I was about to go through the surgery and decided to ask the Doctor can I have a breast reduction because I am tired of carrying these jugs around.

He said, "No, sorry." My mother was laughing at me as she normally does. He then asked, "How can you joke around at this time?" That was my way of facing what was about to occur.

I was expecting the blessings of God to come upon me and overtake me in my situation that day. The more I thought about it, I figured that God was preparing me for something great, but I must hold on.

That was one of the ways for me to hold on by joking around and trusting in my heart that God got me. Let me say this to you. I believe that if your path is more difficult, it is because your calling is higher. You need to know that it's not over until God says it's over.

Start believing again. Start dreaming again. Start pursuing what God put in your heart. You always get tested the most before you progress to the next level. Your birth was not a mistake. Your life has a purpose.

I pray God will restore everything the enemy stole from you. I decree and declare that your latter will be greater than your former. No matter how life happens, you just don't sit around and feel sorry for yourself. Instead we must get up and fight back.

Everything the enemy has stolen, God is going to restore the joy, the peace, the health and the dreams. No matter how many times you get knocked down, you can/will always make a comeback. Listen, God knows how much we can bear. God has promised that all things, not some, all things are going to work out for your good!

1Cor.2:9 says, "Eyes have not seen, Ears have not heard, neither has entered in the heart of man what God has in store for them that love Him!" God is going to do something big in your life.

It's going to be exceedingly, abundantly beyond all that you have asked for or thought about. This is my prayer in Jesus name. Your testimony will be God did it!

He who has begun a great work in you, is faithful to perform it. Whatever God has planned for your life will be accomplished. It doesn't matter what you're dealing with or who is doing you wrong. Whatever is coming against your family and your progress, God is going to execute vengeance. Vengeance is mine said the Lord. Let God handle your light weight. Don't worry God got you beloved.

Everything the enemy has stolen, God is going to restore the joy, the peace, the health, the dreams. Don't underestimate the work that God is doing in your season of waiting.

Pray and get some rest. God is handling whatever you are wrestling with. Listen, things change. People change, friends change, careers change, but God will never change.

And my God will supply every need of yours. Listen, the devil couldn't take you out so he's trying to wear you out. Don't you dare get weary. Hold on the tide is about to turn in your favor!

Some of us forget where we came from. Listen when I was doing chemo not only was God there for me, but my mother had a heart to be there for me as well. I couldn't go up and down the stairs so all I could do at the time was lay on the couch in the front room. This is something I will never forget because she did not have to do that.

She was bringing me food that I could barely eat. Placing a blanket over me from time to time. Sitting with me just to talk. She even prayed with me and for me. I will never forget it. Thank you God! There is nothing like a mother's love. That's why I couldn't pass the opportunity to give back to her when an unexpected situation occurred. I was Honored to be there for her.

Later I began to think about things I did concerning my children at a certain time in my life. Was I there for them like my mother was for me during my time of struggle? Think about it. I am not sure if you remember the stories or even think about it, but your mother carried you for several months before she gave birth to you right?

What an awesome experience to birth a baby that you carried for months. Okay, they were really cute back then but now they are grown and ready to live on their own. Sometimes these grown individuals can open their mouths to say some strong and painful things.

Yes, they are probably still cute but hopefully inside out. They believe they are ready for the world. Parents are you ready to release them like I am? Well it is time to find out.

Now this may not be your story, but honey there was a time in my life when one of my children said they were moving, I simply asked what do you need?

Let's go shopping! How can I help? Yes indeed! So, your parents took care of you until you were grown enough to move out and live on your own. They may let you come back if needed depending on the situation at hand.

Some of you are still there, yeah, I know. Situations are different in some cases of course. Now even though you left the house, if you get in a bind or situation in most cases you can call on your parents to help you, right? But when I think about the fact that you say I am moving now, baby that can cause some of us to jump up and down and sing a song. Yes, we could make a song out of it baby.

Especially when they have caused you sorrow, pain and trouble besides being so cute. Some of you know what I am talking about raising teenagers. Help us with that struggle God. Guess what? We tend to love them unconditionally anyway. Now it is just time for them to grow up and spread their wings, right?

Just tell them I love you! So long bye bye sweetheart. Smooches. Can't wait to see your new place! I BELIEVE and TRUST God that you will be fine. We serve a God of Miracles! Glory to God! Now let us sing...

"I BELIEVE"

So long bye bye, So long bye bye

Now don't get in your feelings. This song was to break the ice so that you can stop being so uptight. Hopefully it caused you to laugh and smile a little bit. Please don't misunderstand me.

Trust me when I say I love my children with all my heart and will do anything in the world for them. Some folk do not want to be real about some situations. Yes honey, give me my medicine. I love laughter.

My family loves to laugh and I joke around with my children all the time. Laughter is good medicine. **Proverbs 17:22 says, "A joyful heart is good medicine, but a broken spirit dries up the bones."** So, don't be so hard on me. This is my story not yours.

There are some cases when the mama was there when no one else was there. C'mon talk to me now. If you say you're hungry what does mama do?

Not only will she feed you but feed you and your babies if you have any, Hello! You may not be a Breast Cancer Survivor, but you are a survivor of life.

I am also a Survivor of LIFE. I would like you to consider that **we all are Survivors!**

I call you a Survivor If you have lived through or endured any type of hardship and keep going in life. For example, some have endured and lived through losing a loved one. I know when I lost my son, I did not want to get out of bed. It took me awhile to stop feeling sorry for myself.

I've always loved dancing and singing and joking around. During that time in my life I did not want to do any of those things. Now I will never get over losing my son, but I thank God for strength to survive while enduring the pain. The joy of the Lord is my strength. I had to get up! I had to start walking again! I had to start living again! I even started dancing again!

Yes, while caretaking for my mother I may dance from time to time and she loves it. She just laughs and I love it. I thank God for giving me a chance to give back to my mother. That means a lot to me.

I'm at a place now where I want to just thank God for loving me through my good and loving me through my bad. My life has not always been peaches and cream. You think? But it makes me happy to bring joy to someone else's life especially my mother.

One thing I know for sure is that God provides despite the mess I have encountered. I say that because I've had some good days. I've had some lonely days and I've had some hills to climb. I've had some weary days and some sleepless nights. But all my good days outweigh my bad days and I certainly won't complain.

Maybe you survived a bad or unhealthy relationship. Been there done that too and trust me when I say I got the Survivor t-shirt baby! No more "Eat the cake Anna Mae!" "I am not having it Ike!" "Either you come correct or stay at home because my life has taken a turn!" To God be the Glory!

Maybe you survived living through a sickness or infirmity such as High Blood Pressure, Diabetes, or Breast Cancer just to name a few.

Now my family has endured such and we even lost loved ones in the process. Listen, being a Survivor is exceptional! Why do I say that? I say that because you are still here, and you did not give up.

Let's look at the definition of a Survivor. Who is a Survivor? A Survivor is a person that copes well with difficulties in their life. What does it mean to be called a Survivor?

What qualities make a Survivor? First, you didn't give up after facing all the difficulties in your life. So, we define a Survivor as a person who copes with a bad situation or affliction and who gets through it. As far as the qualities that makes a survivor lets me know that you have a sense of 3 things.

- Leadership
- Problem Solving
- Etiquette

Leadership represents your attitude or habit of gathering and organizing people. In other words, you know how to hold it together while leading others to that special place of coping and drawing near to God.

Problem solving is the process of finding solutions to difficult or complex issues. The foundation of proper etiquette is behavior that is accepted as gracious and polite in social, professional, and family situations.

In other words, do you have good manners? Or are you going Cuckoo for Cocoa Puffs (Crazy)? Are you the one that likes to snap, crackle and pop off on everybody? I wish I could sit the emoji eyes right here.

Good manners can mean the difference between success and failure in many aspects of life. Etiquette is all about how to conduct yourself beautifully. Look I am not saying that we get it right all the time because we don't. I repeat, good manners can mean the difference between success and failure in many aspects.

To survive something is to live through it or endure it with class. That's you! Anybody that have been through what you've been through would have had a nervous breakdown. I thank God for what He has healed in my life! **I am a Breast Cancer Survivor!** If it wasn't for God, I would have lost my mind!

God also gave me the wisdom to choose not to be or stay in unhealthy relationships! When you know better you do better. You would think we should know better then choose better.

Oh well I guess I missed that class. Trust me when I say it is a new day. Growth is necessary. Now let's move on. Some of you been healed from diabetes.

Some He healed your High Blood Pressure. If it wasn't for God, you would have given up on life. Glory be to God!

God deserves all the Glory! There were times when I almost gave up. I thought to myself, Lord this is too much. I used to think well you are too old and you are just stuck in a place that seems like you are never coming out. It's been too long! People are not believing in you anymore.

You keep thinking it's over because it is taking so long. But in your gut, in your spirit you keep hearing "It Ain't Over!" "You Got Work to Do!" "Don't quit!" It's by His grace and mercy that you are still here.

Don't worry. The plans that God has for you shall come to pass. Continue to proceed with your process. People don't realize that during this process, folk better leave you alone.

They don't realize that you are over here going through storms and focusing on how you are going to pay your rent or mortgage. Also hoping and wishing you could get your hair done. Stop! Let me help somebody right here. Because during that time in my life that is what was on my mind. That was my thoughts.

Let me be clear that really it is not about your hair or your clothes. But it is about your inside. Some of us need to get that thing together. Stop worrying about what people think or say because people look at the outer appearance and God looks at the inside. God searches the heart people. I thought I would slide that in.

I don' know what your issue could be, but you got folk messing with you while you are dealing with stuff. People who are picking on you better leave you alone because you are not rolling by yourself. Glory to God!

Some folks need to tread lightly when it comes to you. Not because you plan to clap back. Help us God. They need to realize that you are packing a punch because you are rolling with God whether you look like it or not!

Whether you sound like it or not! Whether you dress like it or not! Whether folks think you act like it or not. Listen, everybody got a story to tell. I may not travel the way you travel which means that your journey could be different from mine. You think? But let us reach our destiny without trying to bring folks down. Let's cheer one another on in this season survivor.

It does not matter where you live or what type of car you drive. Folk need to leave you alone! (Genesis 12:3 says, I will bless those that bless you and curse those who curse you.) You need to know that families will be blessed through you.

Blessings and Glory and Honor they all belong to you God! Take this time out to give God Praise for being a blessing and keeping you today! Thank you for keeping me, God! I know I got to keep it moving despite the situation.

CHAPTER 2

ROW ROW ROW YOUR BOAT

Listen, in the book of Mark, the disciples had a boat experience. At first, they were rowing gently down the stream when suddenly, they were hit with a storm. The wind was against them. They were in the boat in the middle of the sea and now in the middle of a storm. The disciples were struggling hard because they were rowing against the wind. No more merrily merrily merrily merrily life is but a dream. Life has now turned into chaos.

Mark 6: 46-48

46) And when he had sent them away, he departed into a mountain to pray

47) And when even was come, the ship was in the midst of the sea, and he was alone on land.

48) And he saw them toiling in rowing: for the wind was contrary unto them: and about the fourth watch of the night he cometh unto them, walking upon the sea, and would have passed by them.

How many of you remember when everything was going well for you and you were going on about your merry way enjoying life? Then here comes the struggle. Here comes the storm. Here comes the fight.

I remember something as simple as when I could go every week to get my hair done. Honey, when I lost all my hair and put on a wig for the first time, I thought I would die. I really struggled with that!

I would either put on a scarf or I would wear a wig. People not knowing your story or struggle would look at you and that wig like why she doesn't get her hair fixed. My God! I knew some of the thoughts, but I just kept going and believing God that I could get it done once my hair grows back. We are living in a day and time where people are so opinionated. Don't worry about what the people say. God got you!

Some people take things for granted. I was one of those who took things for granted until the unexpected happened. It was so embarrassing! This was during the time that my hair grew back.

I went from going once a week to several months in between. That humbled me because we tend to take a lot of things for granted at times. Who would of thought that I would be in that place? Not me! How many of you know that it is not about your hair anyway? Help us God!

I saw miracles after miracles concerning that situation. God, I thank you! Even though Jesus seemed absent in the storm, He was watching them just like he watches us. In the fourth watch of the night, Jesus finally came to them. Listen, God may not be early, but He is an on-time God! He will come when the time is right.

There were many times I saw the hand of God in some of my situations or storms. The disciples were toiling while rowing. That is like you trying to fight against your storms.

There will be storms in your life **SURVIVOR!** The rain falls on the just and the unjust. Being a Christian is not a stay out of trouble for free card.

All things work together for the good of them who love the Lord according to the purpose in your life. God has purpose for you and it's going to take a storm to get your faith to the level where He needs it to be to accomplish His will.

Uh oh, somebody didn't like that. Okay, let me explain. First of all, you need to know that we live in a world that has storms as a natural part of life. The bible says God makes it rain on the just and the unjust.

Then there are some storms that we engineer by our own foolishness and disobedience. That's the kind of storm Jonah got into when he tried to flee from the presence of God. (Jonah 1:1-4). Then there are also storms God sends us for growth. Jesus commanded his disciples to get into a boat and go to the other side of the sea. (Matthew 14:22-24).

He knew a storm was brewing but was teaching them a lesson for their development. Be of good cheer and know that God is willing and able to bring you through your storm. We serve a mighty God!

Don't sit around and have a pity party when you should be praising Him. Even though I have been there and done that. Baby, I used to cry out "Lord please get me out of this!" "How long oh Lord?" "Lord I just want to run away from everybody!" But I don't want to get swallowed up like Jonah.

I literally had to learn to trust God no matter the situation. I say that because being emotional will get you nowhere fast. I then started saying, "I can't wait to see how God is going to move in my situation!" Glory to God!

Mark 6: 49-51

49) But when they saw him walking upon the sea, they supposed it had been a spirit, and cried out:

50) For they all saw him and were troubled. And immediately he talked with them, and saith unto them, Be of good cheer: it is I; be not afraid.

51) And he went up unto them into the ship; and the wind ceased: and they were so amazed in themselves beyond measure and wondered.

The disciples were so afraid in the storm that they thought they saw a ghost. They were in a storm and the wind was against them. It was like nothing was working for them and they were even troubled when they saw Jesus. Probably thinking, "Where have you been Jesus?"

"We thought we were about to die out here in this storm." "Glad you finally showed up Jesus!" Y'all know how we get sometimes when we face a storm and you're looking for God to send that person whether friend or family member to show up to help ease the pain.

It seems like they are not showing up fast enough. And when and if they do show up, you look at them and say, "Well, it's about TIME YOU SHOWED UP!" You say this under your breath. "Where have you been?" This is probably what they were thinking during the time of their frustration.

Jesus had to talk to them and tell them do not be afraid I am here for you. Have courage! Keep the faith! Do not doubt, just believe! It's me! And yes, I know some situations can be so frightening at times but stay focused and continue to trust God. As soon as Jesus climbed into the boat, the wind died down. They were stunned, shaking their heads, wondering what was going on. Just keep row row rowing your boat until the Great I Am shows up to calm the storm. Keep row row rowing your boat until you reach your destiny.

Now as I read the text concerning the storm, it reminded me of an incident that happened while in my home. At this time in my life I had moved my mother in with me.

I would always try to look out for my Mother and/or family members. Well, this particular morning I made my Mother breakfast. While she was eating her breakfast, she began to go out on me. It was like she was passing out on me with food in her mouth.

I immediately ran to her and wrapped my arms around her. I tried talking with her and she would not respond. I immediately called 911. They got there very fast. While they were tending to her, I was trying to put clothes on to go to the hospital with her since I had on my pajamas. Next thing I know they were pulling her to the floor and ripped her shirt and began to press on her chest. They were also trying to keep me calm. They said, "Her heart stopped!" "What?!?!"

I probably was looking like I saw a ghost. Please allow me to be transparent with you. I called on God. I began to pray and say No No No not right now God! I knew without a doubt that God was able to keep her. God you can do exceedingly, abundantly more than we could ask or think. So, I just believed that it was not over for her yet. Not knowing what was going to happen next

I do know that God can call us home at any time. I do know that! Especially, with my Mother being in her 80's. By the way, those that know us knows that we call our mom, Mother. Even though you know that God can call us home at any time, you are still never really really ready. A simple truth for me! God has the final say! And God showed up right on time. He showed up! He heard my cry! And now I can serve her like she served me when I went through my chemo. Thank you for the opportunity God!

So, to continue the story, after working with her for a while she finally came back. I was standing outside the ambulance pacing back and forth talking with my God. After patiently waiting for a while, they then gave me a thumbs up and said that she is now talking. Whew! Now that was frightening. I wouldn't wish that type of challenge or storms of life on anybody!

God brought my Mother back to Life y'all!! That was a **MIRACLE!!** Yes, it could have been over. But it ain't over until God says it's over! To God be ALL the Glory!! Listen, we serve a **MIRACLE WORKING GOD!!** Hello somebody! My God is a **Healer!!** My God is a **Way Maker!!** There is **POWER** in the name of **JESUS!!** Yes indeed! Thank you God!! Hallelujah!! I got a song to sing y'all. Let us sing...

"Way Maker"

Way Maker, Miracle Worker,
Promise Keeper...

CHAPTER 3

DESTINY

Your Destiny is Greater than your disaster. What is in you is greater than anything that has happened to you. You can recover because your destiny is Greater.

Philippians 1:6

"Being confident of this very thing, that he which hath begun a good work in you will perform it until the day of Jesus Christ."

Regardless of what you may now see or how you may feel, the truth is, **YOUR GREATEST DAYS ARE AHEAD.** You're not a finished product. You're a miracle in the making. You have not reached your potential. The work God began in you He will finish! What God started in you He will complete!

You may be in the midst of the greatest battle of your life. Hell may have made an all-out attack against you. Maybe you are in the middle of a trial, an affliction, or a setback that you cannot see any way out of. But I have good news for you. God will bring to pass what He has promised you.

No devil in Hell can stop God's purpose and plan for your life from being fulfilled! God didn't bring you this far to forsake you. He has too much invested in you to give up on you now. Hell is not in charge of your life.

You don't belong to the devil. YOU belong to God, Believer! Satan doesn't control your destiny and Hell doesn't have the power to stop you or keep you down! Just as the devil couldn't keep Jesus in the grave, neither can he keep you in the trial, the setback, or the affliction that you may be in now.

Peter said, "It was impossible for death to hold Him." Jesus did not have enough enemies to hold

Him. The Roman soldiers did not have enough power. Even Satan himself could not stop the resurrection. Jesus was destined to go into the grave and He was destined to come out! Glory be to God!

A setback doesn't mean it's over. A setback is positioning you for a comeback! A door shut means a door is about to open. An ending only means that there is getting ready to be a new beginning. The road to destiny consists of endings and beginnings, setbacks and comebacks.

If you are experiencing a great setback at the present time, then get ready to experience a **GREAT COMEBACK!**

Job experienced a great loss. But in the end, the Lord blessed him with twice as much as he had before. His latter was greater than his beginning. God will bring you out of the trial, the affliction, or the setback.

God brought Joseph out of the pit! Israel out of Egypt! Daniel out of the lion's den! The three Hebrew boys out of the fire! And he will bring YOU out! Many are the afflictions of the righteous: but the Lord delivered them out of them ALL! (Psalm 34:19)

Psalms 30:5b

Weeping may endure for a night, but joy comes in the morning.

Romans 8:37.

Nay, in all things we are more than conquerors through him that loved us.

2Corinthians 2:14

Now thanks be unto God, which causes us to triumph in Christ.

No storm is made to last forever, neither should your trial, affliction or setback. Somebody need to be encouraged today. You need to know that no matter what is going on in your life, God can make it all right. But you got to stay strong. I have a song for you. If you know this song, then sing it with me. Let us sing...

"Be Encouraged"

Be encouraged no matter
what's going on...

CHAPTER 4

THE RESCUE IS COMING

How many things do we conquer? All things! How often do we triumph? Always! I know it may be hard to receive right now. I know in the natural you cannot figure this thing out. But the truth of the matter is that God will take what looks like a curse and turn it into a blessing. He will take what the enemy meant for evil and turn it around for your good. Regardless of what you may be going through, you have the promise of that!

I know you may be wondering in this world of pain and hurts, where is God when it hurts? What is God doing when a believer is going through pain, trouble, and hurt in life? There is a lot of pain and suffering in this world that we are living in. Maybe you have been diagnosed with a sickness or you lost your job or a loved one passed away. Maybe your prayers are taking a long time to be answered.

Despite doing your best, your condition is the same. On one side you are God's child doing everything the best you can but on the other side, you don't have an answer to the pain you are going through. Sometimes you ask God, "Where are you God, I am hurting?" "God get me out of this!"

"I know you are able to do exceedingly, abundantly more than I can ask or think!" Yet you are still in that place.

We know the test Shadrach, Meshach, and Abednego went through. When King Nebuchadnezzar asked the people to fall down and worship the golden image he made, they said, "NO!" "Even if we are thrown into the blazing furnace, the God we serve is able to save us from it." "He will rescue us from your hand. But even if he does not, we want you to know king, that we will not serve your gods or worship the image of gold you have set up."

As a result, they were bound and cast into the furnace that was made seven times hotter. As the king and people were watching, there was a fourth person in the fire. Let's see what the king said:

Daniel 3:25-28(NIV)

25) He said, Look! I see four men walking around in the fire, unbound and unharmed, and the fourth looks like a son of the gods."

26) Nebuchadnezzar then approached the opening of the blazing furnace and shouted, "Shadrach, Meshach and Abednego, servants of the Most High God, come out! Come here!" So, Shadrach, Meshach and Abednego came out of the fire,

27) And the satraps, prefects, governors and royal advisers crowded around them. They saw that the fire had not harmed their bodies, nor was a hair of their heads singed: their robes were not scorched, and there was no smell of fire on them.

28) Then Nebuchadnezzar said, "Praise be to the God of Shadrach, Meshach and Abednego, who has sent his angel and rescued his servants!" They trusted in him and defied the king's command and were willing to give up their lives rather than serve or worship any god except their own God.

God is at work in your life even when you do not recognize it or understand it. He's in the storm with you. He's calling you to rise above it. Rise above your situation even though you may feel alone during this time in your life and wait on the Lord.

They that wait upon the Lord shall renew their strength; they shall mount up with wings as eagles; they shall run and not be weary; and they shall walk and not faint. (Isaiah 40:31)

Do you know that an eagle knows when a storm is approaching long before it breaks? When the storm hits, it sets its wings so that the wind will pick it up and lift it above the storm.

While the storm rages below, the eagle is soaring above it. The eagle does not escape the storm. It simply uses the storm to lift it higher. It rises on the winds that bring the storm.

When the storms of life come upon us, we can rise above them by setting our minds toward God. The storms do not have to overcome us. We can allow God's power to lift us above them.

James 1:12(NIV)

Blessed is the man who perseveres under trial because, having stood the test, that person will receive the crown of life that the Lord has promised to those who love him.

Romans 8:28(KJV)

And we know that all things work together for good to them that love God, to them who are the called according to his purpose.

This means that God is working through everything that happens in our lives. No matter what the problem or heartache may be, God will turn it around for you. You must go through the process to go higher. God put you in the process to prune you. You can come out pure as gold.

Job 23:10

But He knows the way that I take (and he pays attention to it). When He has tried me, I will come forth as (refined) gold (pure and luminous).

I want you to know that whatever it is that you are going through, it will not last. It will pass. When it does, who will you give the glory to? There are some things we go through that's only used to point us into the direction of the Father. He wants us to be His through the storms and all. I've come to the realization of just how important it is to give God the Praise, Glory and Honor through all circumstances. Praise is what I do.

Although the fire may seem like it's growing and never ending, I want to encourage you today. God is with you even in the middle of the storm. He will not let you be defeated but **VICTORIOUS!** Trust Him even when you don't understand. After you've done all you can, just stand.

Let me help somebody today. Can I be transparent with you? Somebody may need to hear this. So, after the incident with my Mother when her heart stopped, she was doing just fine and even talking in the ambulance. By the time she got to the hospital and emergency room it was as if nothing happened. Glory be to God!

She was talking like normal. Even the paramedics came back to check on us because she gave us all a scare. I thanked them and gave them a big hug out of appreciation. My God flexed His Power on that day baby! Trust!

How Great is our God! All will see how Great our God is! He is Great and Mighty! We must put our trust in Him. Trusting Him means staying positive, hoping for the best. Do not play the victim. Trusting Him means digging into your bible, pulling out scriptures and believing His Word. It means, letting go of control and putting it in God's hands. Open your ears and heart to what He says. Trusting God means to move by faith and NOT by sight, not your bank account, not other opinions and not sinful temptations.

Remember, the ones who endure through the fire, shall come out as pure gold. Listen, we've come this far by faith, leaning on the Lord. We must praise God in all that we go through. I had to learn to give God the praise in every circumstance. I feel like singing...

"Praise Is What I Do"

Praise is what I do When I want to be close to YOU

Everything will work if you keep a praise on your lips. Never lose your praise. Let the devil hear your praise! Because the enemy can't stand your praise anyway. We must learn to give God praise despite our circumstance. Let the church say Amen. Let the church say Amen again.

Romans 8:38-39

(38) For I am persuaded, that neither death, nor life, nor angels, nor principalities, nor powers, nor things present, nor things to come,

(39) Nor height, nor depth, nor any other creature, shall be able to separate us from the love of God, which is in Christ Jesus our Lord.

Devil you cannot stop us from the love of God. And know this, devil. You cannot stop our praise! Hallelujah! I feel a breakthrough in the Spirit! Thank you God! We owe you our praise God! Glory to God! **I Praise YOU!!!**

CHAPTER 5

STILL HERE

When Paul wrote those verses in the book of Romans, he had been facing some trying times in his life. He had suffered rejection from friends, persecution from the government, and had spent many months of his life in an isolated prison. But regardless of what people or the circumstances of life did to him, Paul was persuaded, he was convinced that nothing that occurs in this life has the power to separate him, the believer, from the love of God.

Just as there are storms in nature, you will discover there are storms of life. While these storms come in many shapes and sizes, all of them are devastating.

Storms like:

- **Financial Storms** "Honey, we are broke."

- **Medical Storms** "Your tests were not good."

- **Marital Storms** "I'm leaving you."

- **Spiritual Storms** "God, where are you?"

- **Job Related Storms** "You are fired!"

- **Emotional Storms** "Sit down, I got bad news."

Is it possible to survive the storms of Life? Absolutely! Without a doubt we all have a story to tell because we are still here. You may have had challenges that seems unbearable, but you are still here. You may have experienced an illness that had you down, but not out, you are still here. Some may have felt the unbearable, heartbreak, rejection, or defeat, but you are still here.

Some may have suffered the loss of loved ones and the pain is still an open wound, but you are still here by the grace of God. Some may have wrestled with an addiction that had the best of you, but you knew that you could beat it. No matter how tough the struggle may have been, if you continued to fight, you knew you would make it. Through it all, you are still here. Some may have counted you out. Some may have wanted you out. Some sought to take you out, but look at you, you can say, "I'm still here!"

No matter what the situation or circumstance, you can trust in God. I don't know about you, but I will trust in the Lord. No matter what, God has been an ever-present help in the time of trouble.

No matter what, God gives you shelter in a storm. You are still here by the grace and mercy of God. Do not give the devil a foothold. And yes, some things can make you angry at times. If you get angry, this is what the bible says to do,

Ephesians 4:26-27

26) BE ANGRY (at sin-at immorality, at injustice, at ungodly behavior), YET DO NOT SIN: do not let your anger (cause you shame, nor allow it to) last until the sun goes down.

27) And do not give the devil an opportunity (to lead you into sin by holding a grudge, or nurturing anger, or harboring resentment, or cultivating bitterness).

In his instruction on dealing with anger/attitude, Paul warns us: "Do not give the devil a foothold by letting your anger fester." Do not start cussing and getting out of your Christian character. You are a new creature in Christ. Do not make it easy for him!

Every Christian is engaged in a fierce, life defining battle with Satan. He is our adversary.

1Peter 5: 8-11

8) Be sober (well balanced and self-disciplined), be alert and cautious at all times. That enemy of yours, the devil, prowls around like a roaring lion (fiercely hungry), seeking someone to devour.

9) But resist him, be firm in your faith (against his attack-rooted, established, immovable), knowing that the same experiences of suffering are being experienced by your brothers and sisters throughout the world. (You do not suffer alone).

10) After you have suffered for a little while, the God of all grace (who imparts His blessing and favor), who called you to His own eternal glory in Christ, will Himself complete, confirm, strengthen, and establish you (making you what you ought to be).

11) To Him be Dominion (Power, Authority, Sovereignty) forever and ever. Amen.

Sometimes we need to be reminded to dress appropriately. Are you wearing your full armor of God?

Ephesians 6:11

Put on the full armor of God (for His precepts are like the splendid armor of a heavily-armed soldier), so that you may be able to (successfully) stand up against all the schemes and the strategies and the deceits of the devil.

Attention! Soldier! Pay attention! Listen, we are not ignorant of the schemes of the enemy. Further, we have power to resist the devil. "Do not give a foothold or opportunity" emphasizes that this is something within our power to control. The devil can only come as close as we allow him. "Resist the devil and he will flee from you."

Even though the devil is cunning, he can never control our will or force disobedience. Satan is not one to lay down his arms and take mercy on us out of pity or generosity. He only flees from those who have the courage and faith to resist him and turn to God's Promise and Power.

We must Man Up (Grow up!) I mean whenever someone gets on your nerves and says something to you that you do not like, or raises their voice at you disrespectfully, then you do not have to give into the enemy tactics by giving them a piece of your mind. You do not have to clap back. Do not get into a yelling match. I must say that I have come a long way in this area, but God is not through with me yet. Help me God!

Now there was a time in my life when that was very difficult for me. And if someone would say or do something to my family or anyone close to me then I would handle that situation.

I would even get upset with folks I speak to that would not speak back to me. I used to think am I invisible or something? What's wrong with you? Did your parents teach you that? God had to work on this chickadee! I'm talking about inside and outside the church. I thank God I am not where I used to be. But I am still a work in progress. I am so grateful to God. I must say that God is a miracle worker. I decided that I must keep going despite some folks stank attitude. And yes, I said **STANK ATTITUDE!** I will not let them stop me. I will not quit.

CHAPTER 6

DON'T QUIT

Some of you may have the urge to quit. That's what the enemy want us to do. I have gone on a job and smiled with an urge to quit. But I refuse to quit. I came close but decided that it is not what God would have me to do. I had to stick it out. Stick it out even when I didn't want to! It's about us making it to the finish line.

You may not be honored or recognized or even appreciated. They may all be talking about you but keep on going. Let's fight together by praying for you, with you and beside you. Just know that you are going somewhere, and the enemy don't like it. In the process of going somewhere God will remove some folk out of your life.

Why? Because when you fail or made a mistake, your so-called friend judged you. It's okay, because they must be removed. You see people look at the outside and God looks at the heart.

1Samuel 16:7 says, "For man looks at the outward appearance, but the Lord looks at the heart." So, move baby move. Get out of my way because I am going with or without you!

I don't know about you, but I fought a good fight! I fought to get out of bed at times. I fought to go to work. I fought with my family. I fought with myself and I lost a lot of things.

I lost friends, money, job, spouse and I even lost my child, but I kept the faith. It's amazing how you can fix other people lives but have a hard time fixing yourself. Even Jesus said, Father can I quit? Nevertheless, not my will, but thine will be done.

Matthew 26:39

Going a little farther, he fell with his face to the ground and prayed, "My Father, if it is possible, may this cup be taken from me. Yet not as I will, but as you will."

During the time of going through what I've gone through, I must keep praying and keep going. I have made some mistakes in my life. You know, I believe I can help somebody because I been through Hell and Back! I cannot relate to stuck up people though. These are they who act like they have never done anything wrong. Excuse me for sneezing, (Aaachoo), but you got some secrets too. Where the real people at?

Not the ones who are trying to tell you how to live your life while living their lives in a mess. Yes, I said a mess! Which reminds me of a dream I had where God said, "Do not eat at the Mess Hall." Isn't that what the military used to call it? Wasn't that the place where they would eat? Help me somebody! God said, do not enter that room and don't let your kids enter the Mess Hall. You are not allowed, so don't follow anybody there. Don't go down, Go up!

There are folks around you that you cannot talk with because they are too busy judging you while they are parlaying or laying up with Tom, Dick, and Harry or Mary, Jane and Charlotte.

There are those who don't have a clue but want to tell you how to live your life as it relates to relationships. Really? I don't think so. I'm trying to get this thing right myself.

I was hoping you could keep it real with me and be an example for me. I don't know about you, but I don't want to talk to the stuck-up folk who act like they never been through anything or done anything wrong. Help me somebody! If that is you, you or you then you need to get away from me. (Aaachoo), excuse me for sneezing, but I am allergic to that type of spirit!

There are those who want to brag on how good their life is while talking about you. No No No, you are barking up the wrong tree Sparky. You can ruff

ruff ruff all day long, but you need to stop all that barking. God knows the stuff that you never talk about. In fact, you have a struggle yourself. You need help just like I need help. Listen, I'm trying to be holy but I'm not innocent.

I know what it means to be messed up and going through all kind of hell and have no one to talk too. **1 Corinthians 15:33 says, "Be not deceived: evil communications corrupt good manners."** And some of you wonder why your manners are corrupt. Talk to you for what? So, you can put me down? So, you can put all my business and everybody else's business in the streets? No No No! Never mind that.

Take your stuck-up self far away from me trying to tell somebody how to dress like you, drive on your level like you, talk like you, smell like you, get in a relationship like you. Some folk don't have the power to deal with what you are going through anyway, because they are too stuck-up! Bragging on how good they got it and how good they are. It's not about how good you are anyway because your goodness is as filthy rags! Hello lights!

God knows the stuff that you never talk about. God knows the inner things you never bring out. The things that you kept secret. I want to talk to some Real Folk! Some of you been through some stuff that qualifies you to help somebody.

People will disqualify you for your mistakes. Learn to pray for folk instead of talking about them. Listen, if God forgives me, I'm not worried about you with your judgmental self! And in that order!

Nevertheless, do not quit because folk are talking about you! Do not quit because you made a mistake! Do not quit because of your struggles! God has a purpose and plan for your life. Do not quit or throw in the towel. Don't you even think about it.

You can make it despite the circumstances. Don't you want to be all that God wants you to be? One way to do that is to learn when tough times come, don't quit, don't give up, do not be deceived, but look up!

Stay consistent. The single characteristic of those who succeed in the challenges of life is this element of consistency. Joseph was thrown in a pit and did not give up. Paul, in jail, did not give up. Daniel, in captivity did not give up. And God did not forget about any of them. What you say? God did not forget about any of them, Okay?

There was a woman dealing with an issue for 12 years. But when she heard about Jesus, she knew the power of God could turn it around. God is not only able, but He's also willing. Just know that God can turn that thing around for you. Whatever it is you have been dealing with for so long, don't quit! I know there may be times that you don't understand but keep believing. Keep the faith. Yes, you may have struggles and disappointments and even felt alone. But I believe that it is turning around for you! It won't always be like this. I got a song for you. Sing this with me...

"Turning Around for Me"

SING PRAISES

ALL GLORY TO GOD

Made with PraiseMyWall.com

Sometimes discouraged but not defeated
It's turning around for me

I decree and declare that it is your season of turn around. I declare that your situation is getting better! Your future is already looking better! If God said it then I Believe it! Glory be to God!

CHAPTER 7

FAITH WALKING

Hebrews 11:6

But without faith it is impossible (to walk with God and) please Him, for whoever comes (near) to God must (necessarily) believe that God exists and that He rewards those who (earnestly and diligently) seek Him.

Faith is the belief and confidence in what you cannot see. You got to see it before you see it, or you never will see it. It was faith that brought me this far and faith won't fail me now. Somebody is pregnant and is about to give birth to their dreams. Somebody needs to write that book, start that business or record that CD. I encourage you today to do what God called YOU to do. No more delays. You can do it, but you must take the first step. You got this! Just do it!

Go ahead and speak life over yourself. I can do all things through Christ who strengthens me. And because he strengthens me, I am forgetting those things which are behind me and pressing forward towards the mark for the prize of a high calling. The prize is in front and not behind.

To walk by faith is to live in the confident expectation of things that are to come. And so, to walk by faith requires that we become familiar with the promises that God has given to us.

The bible is filled with promises for believers. Nothing is more encouraging or nurturing to our faith than reading the promises of God. So how do we walk by faith? To understand how we walk by faith we must first understand where faith comes from. Let's look at the book of Romans.

Romans 10:17(KJV)

So then faith cometh by hearing, and hearing by the word of God.

Now we know that faith comes by hearing the Word of God. We must know that Gods Word is so important for the believer. So now that we know how faith comes, how do we walk in faith? It starts by taking action.

It starts by taking the first step. That sounds simple since none of us remember learning how to walk. We have seen our children learn how to walk though. There are a lot of missteps, a lot of falling, and a lot of getting ahead of themselves.

The same things happen to us. We miss things, we fall, and we get ahead of God. However, in the end, we learn how to walk. The way we start is by taking that first step. The word "can't" should not be in your vocabulary.

If you are going to learn how to walk by faith, you are going to have to lose the idea that you "can't" do something. You can, if God has guided you to do it.

I don't know about you, but I love to travel. When I decide to travel, I make sure that I know where I am traveling to before I reach the destination. It is essential that we know where we are going when we walk by faith.

When we walk by faith, we need to be able to see our destination. This will keep us from being distracted by things and paths along the way that moves us a different direction or from just walking in circles. When you take a flight to your destination you could experience and enter turbulence. This could cause you to go into a motion of agitation. The movements can be unpredictable.

Now your journey may not be all peaches and cream. It may not be a bag of chips and dip on the side. In fact, you may have to go through something. You may have to go through some opposition. Many people have the assumption that if something is from God, it will be easy. That is not the case at all. If it is from God more than likely, you will experience opposition. **Hello Survivor!**

The opposition can come from well-meaning friends, family, or even other Christians. Not everybody in your life is healthy or motivated from a focus of faith.

Think about it. Jesus who is a model for our Christian life, experienced opposition spiritually from Satan in the desert, also from religious leaders of the day.

I cannot tell you how many religious folks have brought me opposition. It's true. Don't think that if something is from God that all you will get is smooth sailing and kudos of affirmation towards your decision. Get ready for opposition.

Many people believe that if it is of God that they will not experience discouragement, fear, or other emotions that are considered negative. Look at Jesus in the Garden of Gethsemane. He was distraught over what was before Him that He sweated drops of blood. He even asked for the path to be changed but still walked forward in faith.

That reminds me of the time when my Mother was being discharged from the hospital after having a stroke. She went through rehab and was doing well but now she could not walk. She told me that she did not want to go into a nursing home. She had a great fear about going into a nursing home. To honor her wishes, we decided to take her home.

I became her Caretaker. Shout out to all the Caretakers because it is not the easiest job in the world. Listen, I love my Mother with all my heart but there were times, while caretaking, that I experienced blood, sweat and tears.

My Mother, my Queen is one of the strongest women I know. No joke! I love to see her smile and hear her laughter. She was constantly speaking life over herself. I love that. She would always say that she was going to walk again. I never doubted that either. As a matter of fact, I would get in agreement with her.

Since the therapy crew stop coming over to the home, God gave me the wisdom to continue the therapy without them. I have to say that we saw progress. Faith without works is dead so we got to work. We know that we serve a miraculous God who can do anything but fail.

Walking by faith involves maintaining focus. So, if Peter was focused on Jesus, he was successfully walking on the water. But when he began to focus on the winds and the waves, he began to sink. What happened? He changed his focus. His faith wavered when he realized what he was doing.

So, if we focus on the difficult circumstances around us and take our eyes off the God we serve, we too may begin to sink. In order to maintain your faith when situations are difficult, focus on the power of God rather than your own inadequacies. Remember the bible says in **Hebrews 13:5, "God will never leave you nor forsake you."**

I knew God called me. I knew I was chosen. That was not a question. I knew God spoke. I knew it would eventually work out. I just continue to speak "Lord do it." I know you are able.

I knew I had heard from God and yet I continued to walk forward even during despair. Do not let your emotions and your feelings today rob you of what God will give you tomorrow. We must continue to walk forward in faith and stay confident that God will complete it.

Philippians 1:6 (NIV)

Being confident of this, that he who began a good work in you will carry it on to completion

Yes, you may get discouraged. Yes, you may see opposition. But who gave you this mission? Who gave you this mandate? Who chose you? Who called you? Was it God that called you or was it Auntie Shirley? Don't let Auntie Shirley get you caught up because she thinks you look good in a suit. Help us Lord! Finally, if you know it was God, then walk by faith and not by sight. Hang in there! Keep the faith! You got this! God is about to do something new!

CHAPTER 8

A NEW THING

Isaiah 43: 18-19

Forget the former things; do not dwell on the past. (Verse 18)

See, I am doing a new thing! Now it springs up! Do you not perceive it? I am making a way in the wilderness and streams in the wasteland. (Verse 19)

God wants to do a new thing in your life. The first step to embracing the new thing what God wants to do in your life is to change your focus. Quit looking behind and start looking ahead. Stop focusing on what they did or didn't do for you. Forget the former things. Do not dwell on the past. When we focus too much on what happened in the past it becomes hard for us to see what God is doing in the present. God is doing something brand new. I'm talking about new open doors and new victories.

If you are continually looking behind, you cannot see where you are going. If you are ever going to move on to new things in Christ, you must learn that you cannot depend on past victories to sustain you. We all have a past and some things are not so good, therefore we need to ask God for forgiveness.

The children of Israel had many victories in their past but now they are in captivity. All their previous victories were doing nothing to set them free. They needed a new work, a new miracle, a new victory or a new thing. First, the question isn't what has God done, but the question is what is God doing in your life right now? Today! What is it that you want him to do in your life right now?

Secondly, in order to move on to new things in Christ, you must know that you cannot allow your past failures to possess you. Do not dwell on the past. Behold I will do a new thing. New things refer to things which you never heard of or planned.

In other words, it will be the first of its kind. New thing means that it has never been done. It's a new work of God. You can't live in your past glories forever. We're talking about blessings which you will enjoy, which you will experience. This will be new to you and to others, beyond imaginations, beyond expectations.

Jeremiah 33:3

Call unto me, and I will answer thee, and shew thee great and mighty things, which thou know not.

We're talking about new mercy, new grace, new life, new compassions and new opportunities. Make room for God to work a new thing in your life. All you must do is surrender to God. Call on Him He will answer you. God can tell you marvelous and wondrous things that you could never figure out on your own.

Forget the former things: do not dwell on the past. See, I am doing A NEW THING! Now it springs forth. Shall you not know it?

Springing forth means the new beginning. Gods unseen power in action. Gods unseen activity in action. God at work. He is saying, forget about your past. Do not dwell on it. Are you ready for things to change? Are you ready for a new beginning? Are you ready for God to do a new thing in your life? Do not remember the former things. Where is your vision? We can't move forward looking out of the rear-view mirror.

God is an ultimate artist to design your life beautifully. Don't you know that? Shall you not know it? God is doing a new thing. Now it shall spring forth. Thank you Lord! How many of you are thankful and grateful to God for giving you chance after chance after chance when you have messed up time after time? I thank My Almighty God for the second, third and fourth chances!!! C'mon somebody! I know I am not alone!

Isaiah 55:6-7

Seek the LORD while he may be found; call on Him while He is near. (Verse 6)

Let the wicked forsake their ways and the unrighteous their thoughts. Let them turn to the LORD, and He will have mercy on them, and to our God, for he will freely pardon (forgive). (Verse 7)

God is saying, don't you know that you are my chosen? I formed you. I redeemed you. I called you by your name. Don't you know that you are precious to me? You are mine. Don't you know you are created and chosen for my glory and my praise. Come on somebody. Oh, taste and see that the Lord is good!

Give thanks unto the Lord. His mercy endures forever. God got us. Keep the faith. Trust in God. The question is not if we have faith, because we all have a measure of faith. Just know that if He did it before, He can do it again! The children of Israel had experienced great spiritual blessings throughout their journey.

You can cultivate a stronger faith by reading the Word and putting the Word to practice. It wouldn't hurt to surround yourself with people of faith. The children of Israel had seen the hand of God at work in and through their lives. We know that fully trusting in God can be hard at times.

Luke 17:5 says, the apostles said to the Lord, "Increase our faith!" That is when Jesus replied in verse 6, if you have faith as small as a mustard seed, you can say to this Sycamine tree, be plucked up by the root and be planted in the sea, and it will obey you. Don't doubt, just believe! Let me say it again. Don't doubt, just believe!

Are there times when it is easier to believe than others? Are there times when it is harder to believe? Let's look at the book of Mark. Let's see if you can relate to the great need of this father a parent who was totally helpless and desperate because an evil spirit tormented his son. He believed on the power of Jesus to help him, but he struggled in that belief. He had his doubts.

Mark 9:21-24

(21) Jesus asked the boy's father, "How long has he been like this?" "From childhood," he answered.

(22) "It has often thrown him into fire or water to kill him. But if you can do anything, take pity on us and help us."

(23) "If I can?" said Jesus. "Everything is possible for one who believes."

(24) Immediately the boy's father exclaimed, "I do believe; help me overcome my unbelief!"

The very best place to go when we have doubts about anything is right to the feet of Jesus Himself. My heart went out to this father who was in desperate need of a breakthrough. I have compassion for him because I can tell he loves his child very much. He couldn't stand to see him suffer. Lord help us today!

I suspect that many of us have brought the needs of loved ones to the Lord in prayer with just that kind of feeling. Lord we hurt with their pain, but we know that there is power in your name Jesus! We are calling on you Jesus. We know that you can break every chain. I hear the chains falling now! Thank you, Jesus!

CHAPTER 9

THE PRICE IS RIGHT

"Come on Down!" "Come on Down_____!"
Put your name on the blank line. I know most of you
know or heard of the game show, "The Price Is
Right." Let me help somebody today as we compare
it to our spiritual walk with God. When your name
is called, and it is your time then you must come on
down. Now most of the contestants are very excited
about their name being called so they jump up and
down and they give high fives everywhere before
they get there.

So now you must get the price right before you
can come up while everybody is watching you and
listening to you. Help me God! Get ready for the

pruning process. Get ready for the gifts to flow. The purpose of pruning is to enhance spiritual growth by removing whatever inhibits spiritual growth. In order to come up, you must come on down. Help me Holy Ghost! What does that mean?

Matthew 2:11

On coming to the house, they saw the child with his mother Mary, and they bowed down and worshiped him. Then they opened their treasures and presented him with gifts.

Are you ready for the gifts? Are you ready for the prizes? Then bow down and worship Him! The spiritual side of this is that we must bow down and worship God. When we humble ourselves and begin to worship, then the gifts will begin to flow. Thank you God!

Once your name has been called and you made it in being a participant in the game (you have been chosen), you now must get the price right. So, let the games begin if you will. Let the praises begin. Bow down and worship Him. Then we can begin to flow with the gifts. Glory to God. You in the house now!

"Come on Down!" Humble yourself! Seek God while you are dealing with the test and trials you may face in life. Bow down in His presence. Seek God while He may be found. Hallelujah! Thank you Jesus! We worship your Holy Name!

Once you humble yourself and bow down and get into the presence of God then you may have to deal with losing some friendships/relationships, deal with being alone, deal with family issues and/or other things assigned to **your humbling experience**.

In other words, let God mold you, prune you, trim you, cut some dead things away from you to increase fruitfulness and growth. Pruning is likening unto a plant for example.

Pruning influences the direction in which a plant grows. Each time you make a cut, you stop growth in one direction and encourage it in another. Trees and shrubs stay healthier if you remove branches that are diseased, dead, pest ridden, or rubbing together. Help us God!

Remember that before you can move to the next level or come up you must get the price right. In other words, there is a price to pay. It may not be easy, but you must pay a price and "Come on Down." Humble yourself. Bow down in His presence.

In other words, it's going to cost you something. I know some of us thought it was going to be a hop, skip and jump. No no no baby! If your name is called, if you are the chosen one, then know that the price must be right to move into purpose. Let the church say Amen. Let the church say Amen again.

Stay encouraged today. Don't give up until you get it right. Some may take longer than others but nevertheless keep moving and keep trying. You must pass the test on each level. You got this! Once you get the price right, then and only then you can now come up to the stage and let the gifts flow. Your latter will be Greater!

CHAPTER 10

PROMISES PROMISES PROMISES

Have you ever been promised anything that you were so excited about and waited and waited and waited? Anticipation was really starting to get to you to a point that even you began to doubt if it was really going to happen. Oh yeah, I'm sure there has been a word spoken over your life about all the great things God had in store for you. But you are yet to see it happen. Just like Zachariah said to the angel, "Do you expect me to believe this?" Let's look at scripture.

Luke 1:12-15 (Message Bible)

(While Zachariah was praying in the sanctuary, an angel of God appeared, and Zachariah was paralyzed in fear)

Verses: 13-15

But the angel reassured him, "Don't fear, Zachariah. Your prayer has been heard. Elizabeth, your wife, will bear a son by you. You are to name him John. You're going to leap like a gazelle (an animal known to move swiftly) for joy and not only you-many will delight in his birth. He'll achieve great stature with God.

Verses: 15-17

"He'll drink neither wine nor beer. He'll be filled with the Holy Spirit from the moment he leaves his mother's womb. He will turn many sons and daughters of Israel back to their God. He will herald God's arrival in the style and strength of Elijah, soften the hearts of parents to children, and kindle devout understanding among hardened skeptics-he'll get the people ready for God."

Verse: 18

Zachariah said to the angel, "Do you expect me to believe this?" "I'm an old man and my wife is an old woman." "Really?"

Verse: 19-20

But the angel said, "I am Gabriel, the sentinel of God, sent especially to bring you this glad news. But because you won't believe me, you'll be unable to say a word until the day of your son's birth. Every word I've spoken to you will come true on time-God's time."

So, to make a long story short, Zachariah continued speechless and had to use sign language with the people until his wife conceived. Wow! I wonder what that was like. I mean after all him and his wife was believing and trusting God for a long time.

So here you have Zachariah and Elizabeth who were good people. Righteous before God, living blamelessly but what was not happening for them was a baby. They were childless! For years they had lived with the stress and grief of wishing for a baby but being disappointed.

And they had to deal with people talking about them saying things like, "I thought they were a child of God so where is their baby they been praying for?"

"If children are a blessing from God, then they must be going through punishment for some sin they did." People still say the most hurtful things.

And yet, though they had no child, Zechariah and Elizabeth kept the faith. Not everyone would have kept the faith like they did. Zechariah and Elizabeth stayed faithful even though there seem to be no reward for it. Though they had not been blessed with a baby, they kept believing in God's faithfulness. How do you keep faith in God despite heart-wrenching disappointment?

Evidently, they hung in there despite what it looked like. Despite what their eyes couldn't see. I don't care what it looks like people, we must continue to trust and believe God. Now this is easier said than done. Yeah, I know you may be one of those Super Christians who always got it together and never do anything wrong and who has never doubted anything. If that is you, then I am not talking to you. But the rest of us need to do better by preparing ourselves.

God is faithful to keep His promises. Believers we are called to cling to the promises of God because we trust the God who made the promise in the first place. Hello somebody! Keep fighting until your victory is won. Keep standing on the promises of God. He will come through, no doubt. Prepare yourself for the promise.

CHAPTER 11

PREPARE

Listen, when the angel appeared to Zachariah, he was calling him to prepare. It was now time for Zachariah and Elizabeth to prepare to have a baby. And the baby would become a prophet who would prepare the people for the Lord. So, it was a call to prepare.

Zachariah was completely unprepared for this and said, "You expect me to believe this?" "How can I be sure of this?" "I'm old and my wife is well along in years too." And this was NOT the right thing to say because after he said that the angel shared his credentials and read him his rights.

"I am Gabriel. I stand in the very presence of God. I was sent to speak to you and to tell you this good news. And now you will be silent and not be able to speak until the day this happens because you did not believe my words, which will come true at the appointed time."

Ooooweeee. We are talking now 9 months of preparation! Imagine that. A preacher who can't talk. What you say?

- Nine months for a persons' words to be silenced

- Nine months to ponder the meaning of what he had seen and heard from the angel

- Nine months to think about his response to the angel

- Nine months to understand what God would be doing with their son whom the angel said to name him John

- Nine months of sign language

It is no more "Do you understand the words that are coming out of my mouth jokes." This is the real deal! It is, "No talking in class." "Raise your hand if you're sure." Because the math problem you're working on at this time will be solved in 9 months. Help us God! It's complicated but you must prepare. Let's look at scripture to see how Elijah prepared for what was to come in their situation.

1 Kings 18: 41-45

We're told that Elijah said to Ahab, "Go up, eat and drink, for there is a sound of the abundance of rain." So, Ahab went up to eat and to drink. And Elijah went up to the top of Mount Carmel. And he bowed himself down on the earth and put his face between his knees. And he said to his servant, "Go up now, look toward the sea."

And he went up and looked and said, "There is nothing there." Seven times Elijah said, "Go back." The seventh time the servant reported, "A cloud as small as a man's hand is rising from the sea. So, Elijah said, "Go and tell Ahab, 'Hitch up your chariot and go down before the rain stops you.' Meanwhile, the sky grew black with clouds, the wind rose, a heavy rain started falling and Ahab rode off to Jezreel. The power of the LORD came on Elijah and, tucking his cloak into his belt, he ran ahead of Ahab all the way to Jezreel.

This is an example of how to pray like Elijah prayed. How can we shake the heavens and bring down the abundance of rain of God's blessings? Notice Elijah's posture. First, he humbled himself. He not only prayed humbly but he prayed specifically.

Sometimes our prayers are too general. Prayers like, "Lord bless all the Deacons." Exactly how are you going to know if that prayer has been answered.

Elijah knew what he wanted. He specifically asked for rain. He not only prayed specifically but he prayed with expectation. He also prayed persistently. Then it came to pass the seventh time. How great is our God! Let's sing together...

"How Great Is Our God"

How Great is Our God...?

Chapter 12

EXPECTATION

Let's look back at our childhood for a moment. Remember how you were the night before Christmas or maybe your Birthday. Honey you were excited and filled with expectation and anticipation. Super excited to the point that you could hardly control yourself. You had trouble falling asleep and it felt like your heart was running overtime. You couldn't wait until you were able to open your presents and see what you got. Now that's expectation!

Let's define expectation:

Expectation is a strong belief that something will happen or be the case of the future. It is a belief of what can realistically be achieved or delivered.

If you want something to happen in your life you must expect for that thing to happen. Some people go to church just to go to church out of tradition. They have no sense of expectation and no desire to see God manifest Himself.

So, they walk out of the church exactly as they came in because there was not an expectation for anything. **Having a form of godliness but denying the power thereof. 2Tim 3:5.**

I don't know about you, but I walk in expectation. There are promises of blessings all in the bible. Remember Jesus said, "The thief comes only to steal and to kill and destroy, I come that you may have life, and have it to the full (more abundantly.) We are talking a better life than you ever dreamed of. I expect that life.

I expect good things to come my way. When I pray, I expect something to happen. When I give, I expect something to happen. Do you have that expectation? The promises of God for you are real when we are in relationship with a true and living God. We must believe and have faith.

If you don't believe that it's the will of God for you to be healed, to be delivered, to prosper, to live life abundantly then it's highly doubtful you'll expect it. What are your expectations?

God can do more in your life and mine than we can hope or think or imagine. There may be many things we cannot do in our own strength or our own ability but **with God, Nothing is Impossible!**

Let's look at the bible to encourage your expectation:

Matthew 18:19

"I also tell you this: If two of you agree here on earth concerning anything you ask, my Father in heaven will do it for you.

Matthew 21:22

You can pray for anything, and if you have faith, you will receive it.

Mark 11:24

Therefore, I say unto you, Whatsoever you desire, when you pray, believe that you receive them, and you shall have them.

John 15:7

If you abide in me, and my words abide in you, you shall ask what you will, and it shall be done unto you.

John 14:13

And whatsoever you shall ask in my name, that will I do, that the Father may be glorified in the Son.

1 John 5: 14-15

(14) This is the confidence we have in approaching God: that if we ask anything according to His will, He hears us.

(15) And if we know that He hears us, whatever we ask, we know that we have what we asked of Him.

When we pray, we need to pray in faith and we need to expect God to do exceedingly, abundantly above all things that we ask or think. Expectation is the characteristic of true faith. **Hebrews 11:1 tells us "Now faith is the substance of things hoped for, the evidence of things not seen."**

Hope in the bible is describing something you can count on. Something you can bank on. We live with great expectations in a God who loves us and promises that the work that He has started in our lives, He will complete. Is there anything too hard for God? **There is NOTHING too hard for God!** Remember that!

CHAPTER 13

WORD UP!

(WORDS FRAME YOUR WORLD)

Do you have a situation that you want to change? Is there anything you want to make or see in your life? You don't have to cry about it. You can take the word of God and use it to change things or recreate your world for the better. Word up! This is the principle that God used to create the world!

And God said, Let there be light: and there was light. (KJV) Genesis 1:3

Through faith we understand that the worlds were framed by the word of God, so that things which are seen were not made of things which do appear. (KJV) Heb 11:3

By faith, we see the world called into existence by God's Word, what we see created by what we don't see. (MSG) Heb 11:3

By faith we understand that the universe was formed at God's command, so that what is seen was not made out of what was visible. (NIV) Heb 11:3

What do you want to create today? What situation do you want to change? That word that created the universe and upholds it today is still here with us. Take it with you and lift your voice in prayer to God. In other words, send the Word of God up! Word up! When you have incubated upon that situation, go ahead and speak and recreate your world!

What am I saying? I am saying when a chicken sits on an egg, it incubates it. To incubate means to keep something safe and warm so that it can grow. You incubate a plan or an idea before bringing it into the world, or, metaphorically speaking, hatching it. Speak and recreate your world.

Here are some examples of how to take a problem you are facing and find scripture on the subject and personalize the verses for daily confessions. Come on say something to recreate your world. Send the Word up!

(Fear)

Fear not: for I have redeemed thee, I have called thee by thy name; thou art mine. (Isaiah 43: 1b)

The Lord is my light and my salvation; whom shall, I fear? The Lord is the strength of my life; of whom shall I be afraid? Though a host should encamp against me, my heart shall not fear; though war should rise against me, in God I will be confident. (Psalm 27:1, 3)

(Worry)

Be careful for nothing; but in everything by prayer and supplication with thanksgiving let your requests be made known unto God. And the peace of God, which passes all understanding, shall keep your hearts and minds through Christ Jesus. (Philippians 4:6-7)

Peace I leave with you; My (perfect) peace I give to you; not as the world gives do, I give to you. Do not let your heart be troubled, nor let it be afraid. (Let My perfect peace calm you in every circumstance and give you courage and strength for every challenge.)   (John 14:27)

(Entrepreneurship)

Trust in the Lord with all your heart; do not depend on your own understanding. Seek His will in all you do, and He will show you which path to take. Don't be impressed with your own wisdom. (Proverbs 3:5-7)

Honor the Lord with your wealth and with the first fruits of all your crops (income); Then your barns will be abundantly filled. (Proverbs 3:9-10)

Blessed (fortunate, prosperous, and favored by God) is the man who does not walk in the counsel of the wicked (following their advice and example), Nor stand in the path of sinners, Nor sit (down to rest) in the seat of scoffers (ridiculers).

But his delight is in the law of the Lord, And on His law (His precepts and teachings) he (habitually) meditates day and night. And he will be like a tree firmly planted (and fed) by streams of water, which yields its fruit in its season; Its leaf does not wither; And in whatever he does, he prospers (and comes to maturity). (Psalms 1:1-3) (Amplified Version)

(Marriage)

Summing up: Be agreeable, be sympathetic, be loving, be compassionate, be humble. That goes for all of you, no exceptions. No retaliation. No sharp-tongued sarcasm. Instead, bless--that's your job, to bless. You'll be a blessing and also get a blessing. Whoever wants to embrace life and see the day fill up with good, here's what you do: Say nothing evil or hurtful; Snub evil and cultivate good; run after peace for all you're worth. (1 Peter 3:8-11) (Message Version)

(Sickness)

But He was wounded for our transgressions, he was bruised for our iniquities: the chastisement of our peace was upon him; and with his stripes we are healed. (Isaiah 53:5)

Many are the afflictions of the righteous, but the LORD delivers him out of them all. (Psalms 34:19)

He sent His word, and healed them, and delivered them from their destructions. (Psalms 107:20)

Is any sick among you? Let him call for the elders of the church; and let them pray over him, anointing him with oil in the name of the Lord: And the prayer of faith shall save the sick, and the Lord shall raise him up; and if he have committed sins, they shall be forgiven him. (James 5:14-15)

The Bible has much to say about how we manage our words. Your ability or inability to control your tongue will determine more than anything else the level of success you enjoy in your relationships. If you can't seem to say the right thing and you constantly seem to say the wrong thing in a relationship, you just might find yourself alone and alienated from everyone in your life.

Some people find it so easy to express themselves and have no trouble saying what is on their mind. Some may refer to these people as brilliant conversationalists.

Some of them can talk on and on and on to the break of dawn and never get around to really saying anything at all. But we all know there is more to speaking effectively than being able to string words together

The words we speak have power. They are more powerful than many people realize. The words we say can put a smile on someone's face or bring tears to another one's eyes. We can encourage one another with the words we speak, or we can crush the hopes and dreams of the ones we love by not watching what we say. Come on Word up!

We are told in Hebrews 11:3 that the very world in which we live in was framed by the word of God. Several times in Genesis we read the words

"And God **SAID** let there be...and it was."

Speaking faith-filled words is God's way to bring things into existence. And we are created in His very own IMAGE. So just like a child imitates his parents so should we as God's children imitate our heavenly Father who created us in His IMAGE and LIKENESS.

We can speak things out of ignorance. Ignorance can be a fundamental problem. Let's look at Hosea 4:6, and Is. 5:13.

My people are destroyed for lack of knowledge. Because you have rejected knowledge, I also reject you... (Hosea 4:6)

What God is saying is people are being destroyed because they don't know me! They don't know me, and they refuse to know me. So, if you refuse to know Him then He will not recognize you as His priests. C'mon let's get it together and walk in the likeness of our heavenly Father.

> *Therefore, my people are gone into captivity, because they have no knowledge. (Isaiah 5:13)*

Are you sick of being held captive? A person can be held captive and not even realize it. You can be held captive just by the way you think and not even realize that you are. You can be held captive just by the way you speak and not even realize it.

The devil wants to hold you captive and keep you away from God. God wants to set you free and give you peace of mind. God will give you back everything that the devil stole from you. Are you ready to do it God's way and receive peace of mind by sending **His Word Up?** Remember God wants to give you back everything that the devil stole from you and much more! Jehovah Shalom, He is my Peace. Glory to God.

CHAPTER 14

SPEAK RIGHT!!!

Speaking right words are important! Let's look at (Job 6:24-25)

"Teach me, and I will hold my TONGUE: and cause me to understand wherein I have erred: HOW FORCIBLE ARE RIGHT WORDS..." (In other words, confront me with the truth and show me where I went wrong, and I will shut my mouth. Make me understand how I have gone off the track.)

Some of us need to be reminded or told once, twice or even more times to watch what we say. Now normally you will never out right just tell someone to shut up without them getting offended. But just let me take the role of Big Mama right now.

We hope you don't get offended while we allow Big Mama to put us ALL in our place. Tell us Big Mama! "Shut your mouth!" "Shut up, I said Shut up you talk too much!" "You got a Big Mouth, oh boy you Never Shut Up!"

"Keep talking, I am about to wash your mouth out with soap!" How many of your parents ever told you that?

Now there are times when we need to be quiet and there are times when we need to speak life or positive if you will. The words we speak have power. They are more powerful than many people realize.

I don't know about you, but I like to make people smile or give them laughter even when they are dealing with life that could cause one to be down and out. I have learned that laughter has helped me to survive the chaos I was dealing with. Remember that a joyful heart is good medicine, but a broken spirit dries up the bones. (Proverbs 17:22) Give me my medicine!

We must learn to speak life and not death over someone's life. Your words determine your destiny. The word of God has Creative Power. We must boldly speak the promises of God by Faith.

Death and life are in the power of the tongue: and they that love it shall eat the fruit thereof. (Proverbs 18:21)

Words bring about change in our lives. Words set the direction of our life. Learn to speak faith, not feelings. Speak destiny, not despair. Speak health not sickness. Baby I believe that people who are married need to consider this scripture on a daily basis.

So many people are hurting in their marriages today. This simple, yet powerful scripture, can help married couples enrich their relationships and find peace in troubled times. Our words are seeds. Every word we speak will carry a harvest with it whether good or bad. We choose life and death with our words which are seeds. We need to take responsibility for our words. What is our mouth producing?

Your marriage will never be better than your mouth. I can talk about it because I've been there. Help me Holy Ghost. What's in our hearts will come out of our mouths. **WORDS MATTER!** By our words we are justified or condemned. If you want to change your life, change your talk.

If you want to change your marriage, then try starting with changing your talk. If you want to strengthen a friendship, start with your talk. If you want people to treat you better at work, start with your talk. People say some rough and tough things sometimes but be very careful what YOU say

YOU REAP WHAT YOU SOW! Words are seeds. Let's read the bible.

1 Peter 3:7

Husbands, in the same way be considerate as you live with your wives and treat them with respect as the weaker partner and as heirs with you of the gracious gift of life, so that nothing will hinder your prayers.

Come on somebody. He over there talking crazy to his wife and wondering why his prayers is not being answered. Wondering why his prayers are being hindered. Now if this is not you, then I am not talking to you. But I got to help somebody today. Well, what did you say to your wife, the gift that God gave you? How did you talk to her?

Then you slide on up in the church like nothing ever happened. Really? Check yourself before you wreck yourself! We got to do better people. If you know better, then do better. Now I know we got some good brothers out there, but somebody need to hear this. Let the church say Amen. Let the church say Amen again.

Hold up! It ain't over. Let's talk to the wives for a minute. What does the bible say to the wives? Especially when some of us are always talking about respect. I know I did at a certain time in my life. And still today looking for respect!

To be honest I was not ready. I say that because I know now that marriage is work. I'm talking about a job like no other! Help me Holy Ghost! I was not ready to put in the work with all the junk and baggage that I was carrying. I tried but I couldn't do it. Maybe that was the problem is that I tried. Help me God!

1 Timothy 3:11

In the same way, the women are to be worthy of respect, not malicious talkers but temperate and trustworthy in everything.

You know some of us had to understand it by and by. Because being from the hood can cause you to have a mouth on you. Thank God for growth. I can hear some of you singing Aretha Franklin's song Respect right now just as loud as you can. R.E.S.P.E.C.T. find out what it means to me! Do you know what it means? Do you have self-control? Do you really know who you are?

Let me remind you so that you can start speaking right! Let that brother have his peace! Now let me speak life over you sister. You are Beautiful! You are

Valuable! When you know these things, your love flows more freely. Do you know who you are?

You are clothed with strength and dignity! You open your mouth with wisdom and the teaching of kindness is on your tongue! You are worth far more than rubies! You are fearfully and wonderfully made! I am one that watches married couples all the time. Maybe we can learn something from them. One thing I know for sure is that I am worthy of respect so don't bring me any mess. I thought that I would just slide that in. Thank you! Hallelujah! Speak right people! Glory to God!

CONCLUSION

2 Corinthians 5:7

"For we walk by faith, not by sight."

Those words seem simple enough. However, I am learning that it requires tremendous courage and strength. You must be willing to be misunderstood and even abandoned. You must be willing to look like a complete fool. I must confess that it is a journey of tremendous blessing and reward. It is a journey that is exciting, life altering and mind-boggling. It is a journey that will allow you to see and experience God as he was meant to be in all His fullness and grace.

Walking by faith and not by sight requires you to go to a place you do not know. One that God will reveal as you walk in obedience. Walking by faith means that you continue to cling to the dreams God has planted in your heart, even when you've been thrown in a pit, or taken to prison for crimes you didn't commit.

Just look at all Joseph endured after telling his family about his dream. He was favored by his father and hated by his brothers. Joseph was sold into slavery by his own jealous brothers. He gains favor with his Egyptian Master, Potiphar, which makes Joseph the most powerful man under his authority.

Joseph remains faithful by rejecting his master's wife advances that angers her and causes Joseph to be imprisoned on false charges. Eventually, Joseph is elevated to the second highest position in the land, and then God uses a famine to bring his brothers to Egypt. Joseph has the perfect opportunity to get revenge but does not do so. Joseph's dealings with his brothers will eventually bring them to repentance and thus they will be reconciled as a family.

Walking by faith requires a strong determination to follow God's plan regardless what life throws your way. It means you have the courage to stand up for the hurting or broken. You just may have to play the part of a fool. Think about Noah building an ark for a flood when it had never ever rained on earth.

Think about Abraham clinging to the promise that he would be the father of many nations even though he was childless at the age of 100.

Think about Moses standing before the Israelites in the wilderness telling them they would eat manna until it disgusted them but having no idea where that manna would come from. Think about Joshua marching around the walls of Jericho as God had told him to and wondering what good it was going to do.

If you choose this path, you must be willing to get out of your comfort zone. You must be willing to let God take your world and turn it upside down, shake it up, and do a new thing in your life. I don't know what your shake up might look like, but I know if you surrender and give it to God, God can change your life for the better.

Just know you are not alone. God is raising up a remnant of believers who will be obedient. He is looking for those with a pure heart. He is looking for those who is willing to choose obedience even if it costs them everything this world has to offer. He is looking for those who will cling to His promises even when it seems there is no hope.

God has chosen you to be a part of this remnant. This is those who will allow him to take their lives and mold them into what He wants. He has chosen you to have your faith tested and tried, and yet promises that the fire will only purify you-not burn you.

He promised that He will never leave you nor forsake you. He has promised that He will be with you every single step, walking with you, carrying you, supporting you. God is still in control even when it doesn't look like it.

Be strong and courageous. He is teaching you to trust Him so He can do something bigger and better than you ever dreamed possible. He is teaching you to let go and trust Him with your heart, your soul, your life.

He is teaching you to walk in the spirit so He can do even greater works in you and through you. He is preparing you to be that light to a world that needs to see Jesus

I don't know where you are on this journey of walking by faith, but I encourage you to surrender. Let God take your life, your pain, your loss and use it for His glory. Ask Him to do an amazing work in you so he can do an amazing work through you. Delight yourself also in the Lord, and He shall give you the desires of your heart. (Psalms 37:4.) You might as well shout before you get it.

Get out of that boat and step onto the water and never take your eyes off Jesus. It is a decision you will never regret! I got a song for you. Feel free to look this song up on YouTube to follow along. Great song. Listen to the words. Let us sing...

"BIG"

I Believe That it's my Season

And it's going to be Big!

Listen, what's in front of you is bigger than what's behind you. Praise God! Hallelujah! I believe that it's your season! I believe that it's my season! I am excited about your future! I'm excited about my future. My promise is Big! What about yours? Go ahead and praise Him before it happens! Glory to God! I know He's able! I surrender God!

SURRENDER TODAY

Surrendering to God is showing complete faith in Him and belief in His promises. Just like a child, we can walk in freedom from worries. We simply must choose to trust God for everything. If we can trust God for our salvation through Jesus Christ, we can trust Him for our daily needs and desires. Surrendering means that you completely give up your own will and subjects your thoughts, ideas and deeds to the will and teachings of God. Submit yourself today. God is waiting with open arms.

Matthew 18:3

"Truly I tell you, unless you change and become like little children, you will never enter the kingdom of heaven."

Matthew 6:34

"Therefore, do not worry about tomorrow, for tomorrow will worry about itself."

Don't worry about tomorrow because today is the day that your new life begins. God did not create you to worry. God did not create you to fear. But he created you to worship Him daily. He is Jehovah Jireh, God our Provider. He is willing and able to provide for you.

This is the day that the Lord has made. We will rejoice and be glad in it. God is so merciful, and He cares for you. I am excited about your future. We realize that you are human, and you don't have all the answers or control, no matter how awesome and capable you are. Just take a moment. Admit that you don't have to have all the answers all the time. Take a deep breath. Fear not! Now pray this prayer with me.

Prayer:

Heavenly Father, I come humbly before your throne. I know that I am a sinner, please forgive me. I repent. I believe Jesus died for my sins and rose from the dead. I turn from my sins and invite You to come into my heart and life. I ask you to be my Lord and Savior.

To God be the Glory! If you prayed this prayer, then today is going to be a new day of Victory for you! Welcome into the heavenly Kingdom! The Angels are rejoicing in heaven. I am excited about your new journey!

Luke 15:10

In the same way, I tell you, there is joy in the presence of the angels of God over one sinner who repents.

"Amazing Grace"

AMAZING GRACE HOW SWEET
THE SOUND THAT SAVED
A WRETCH LIKE ME

Jesus Christ is the Light of the world.
His truth will set you free. Jesus is the Way the Truth
and the Life.

AUTHOR CONTACT

Email Address:

sheridsmith@hotmail.com

You're welcome to send your prayer requests. Please include your testimony and indicate how this book has blessed you when you write.

Thanks for reading!

Please add a review on Amazon and let me know what you thought!

Amazon reviews are extremely helpful for authors, thank you for taking the time to support me and my work. Don't forget to share your review on social media with the hashtag #HelloSurvivor and encourage others to read my journey too!